DRAW 50 MAGICAL CREATURES

BOOKS IN THIS SERIES

Draw 50 Princesses
The Draw 50 Way
Draw 50 Airplanes, Aircraft, and Spacecraft
Draw 50 Aliens, UFOs, Galaxy Ghouls, Milky Way Marauders, and Other Extraterrestrial Creatures
Draw 50 Animal 'Toons
Draw 50 Animals
Draw 50 Athletes
Draw 50 Baby Animals
Draw 50 Beasties and Yugglies and Turnover Uglies and Things That Go Bump in the Night
Draw 50 Birds
Draw 50 Boats, Ships, Trucks, and Trains
Draw 50 Buildings and Other Structures
Draw 50 Cars, Trucks, and Motorcycles
Draw 50 Cats
Draw 50 Creepy Crawlies
Draw 50 Dinosaurs and Other Prehistoric Animals
Draw 50 Dogs
Draw 50 Endangered Animals
Draw 50 Famous Caricatures (out of print)
Draw 50 Famous Cartoons
Draw 50 Famous Faces
Draw 50 Flowers, Trees, and Other Plants
Draw 50 Holiday Decorations
Draw 50 Horses
Draw 50 Monsters, Creeps, Superheroes, Demons, Dragons, Nerds, Dirts, Ghouls, Giants, Vampires, Zombies, and Other Curiosa . . .
Draw 50 People
Draw 50 People from the Bible
Draw 50 Sharks, Whales, and Other Sea Creatures
Draw 50 Vehicles

DRAW 50 MAGICAL CREATURES

THE STEP-BY-STEP WAY TO DRAW UNICORNS, ELVES, CHERUBS, TROLLS, AND MANY MORE

Lee J. Ames
and
Andrew Mitchell

BROADWAY BOOKS
NEW YORK

PUBLISHED BY BROADWAY BOOKS

Published in the United States by Broadway Books, an imprint of The Crown Publishing Group, a division of Random House, Inc., New York.

www.broadwaybooks.com

BROADWAY BOOKS and its logo, a letter B bisected on the diagonal, are trademarks of Random House, Inc.

Library of Congress Cataloging-in-Publication Data
Ames, Lee J.
Draw 50 magical creatures : the step-by-step way to draw unicorns, elves, cherubs, trolls, and many more / Lee J. Ames and Andrew Mitchell. — 1st ed.
p. cm. — (Draw 50 magical creatures)
1. Fantasy in art. 2. Drawing—Technique. I. Mitchell, Andrew J., 1967–
II. Title. III. Title: Draw fifty magical creatures. IV. Series.

NC825.F25A44 2009
743'.87—dc22

2009004905

ISBN 978-0-7679-2799-4 (HC)
ISBN 978-0-7679-2800-7 (TP)

PRINTED IN THE UNITED STATES OF AMERICA

10 9 8 7 6 5 4 3 2 1

First Edition

For Alison Sally, Jonathan David, and their families and pets . . .

To the Reader

Before you begin drawing, here are some tips on how to use and enjoy this book:

When you start working, use clean white bond paper or drawing paper and a pencil with moderately soft lead (HB or No.2). Have a kneaded eraser on hand (available at art supply stores). Choose any one of the subjects in the book that you want to draw and then very lightly and very carefully sketch out the first step. As you do so, study the finished step of your chosen drawing to sense how your first step will fit in. Make sure the size of the first step is not so small that the final drawing will be tiny, or so large that you won't be able to fit the finished drawing on the paper. Then, also very lightly and very carefully, sketch out the second step. Carefully focus on each step to see how it fits into both the previous, and the following step. You must also focus on the final drawing to see how each step is a part of it. As you go along, step by step, study not only the lines but also the size of the spaces between lines. Remember, the first steps must be constructed with the greatest care. A wrongly placed stroke could throw the whole drawing off.

As you work, it is a good idea to have a mirror available. Holding your sketch up to the mirror from time to time can show you distortions you might not see otherwise.

As you are adding to the steps, you may discover that they are becoming too dark. Here's where the kneaded eraser becomes particularly useful. You can lighten the darker penciling by strongly pressing the clay-like eraser onto the dark areas.

When you've put it all together and gotten to the last step, finish the drawing firmly with dark, accurate strokes. There is your finished drawing. However, if you want to further finish the drawing with India ink, applied with a pen or fine brush, you can clean out all of the penciling with a kneaded eraser after the ink completely dries.

Remember, if your first attempts do not turn out too well, it's important to keep trying. Practice and patience do indeed help. I would like you to know that on occasion when I have used the steps for a drawing from one of my own books, it has taken me as long as an hour or two to bring it to a finish.

—Lee J. Ames

DRAW 50 MAGICAL CREATURES

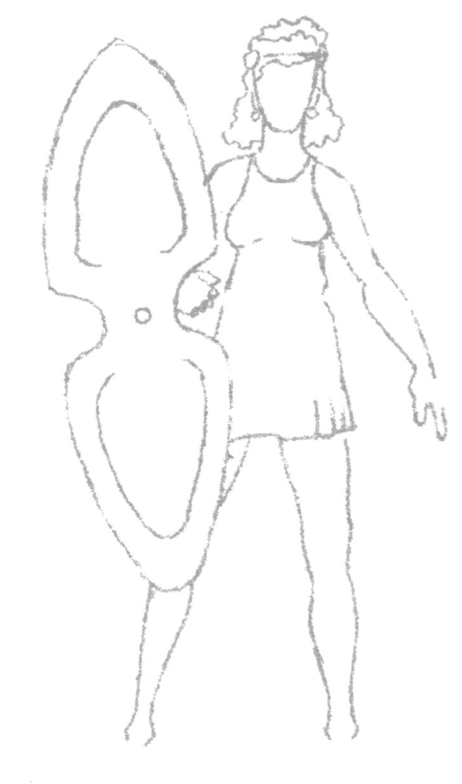

Amazon

Angel

Cherub

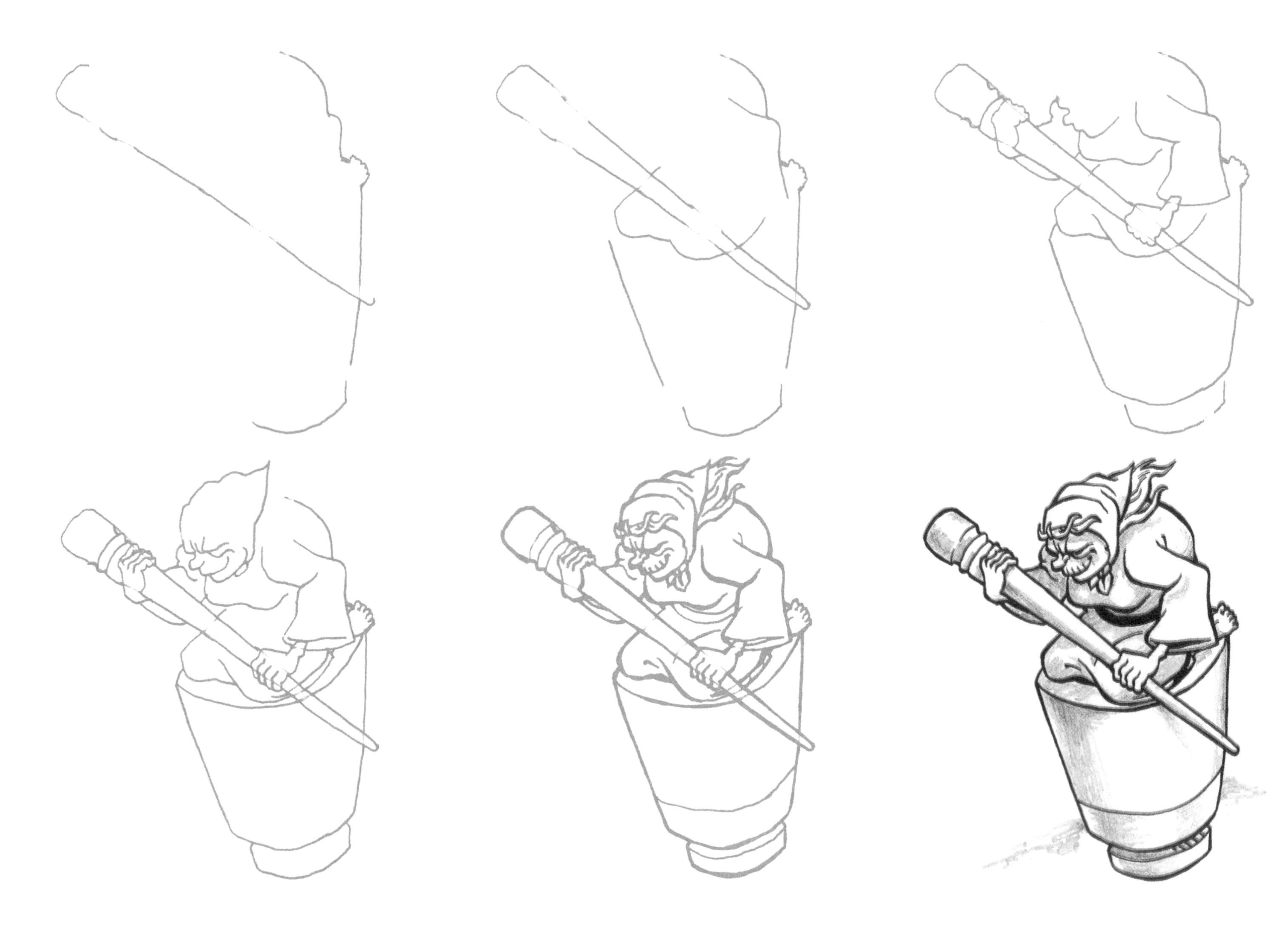

Baba Yaga

Bad Witch

The Good Witch

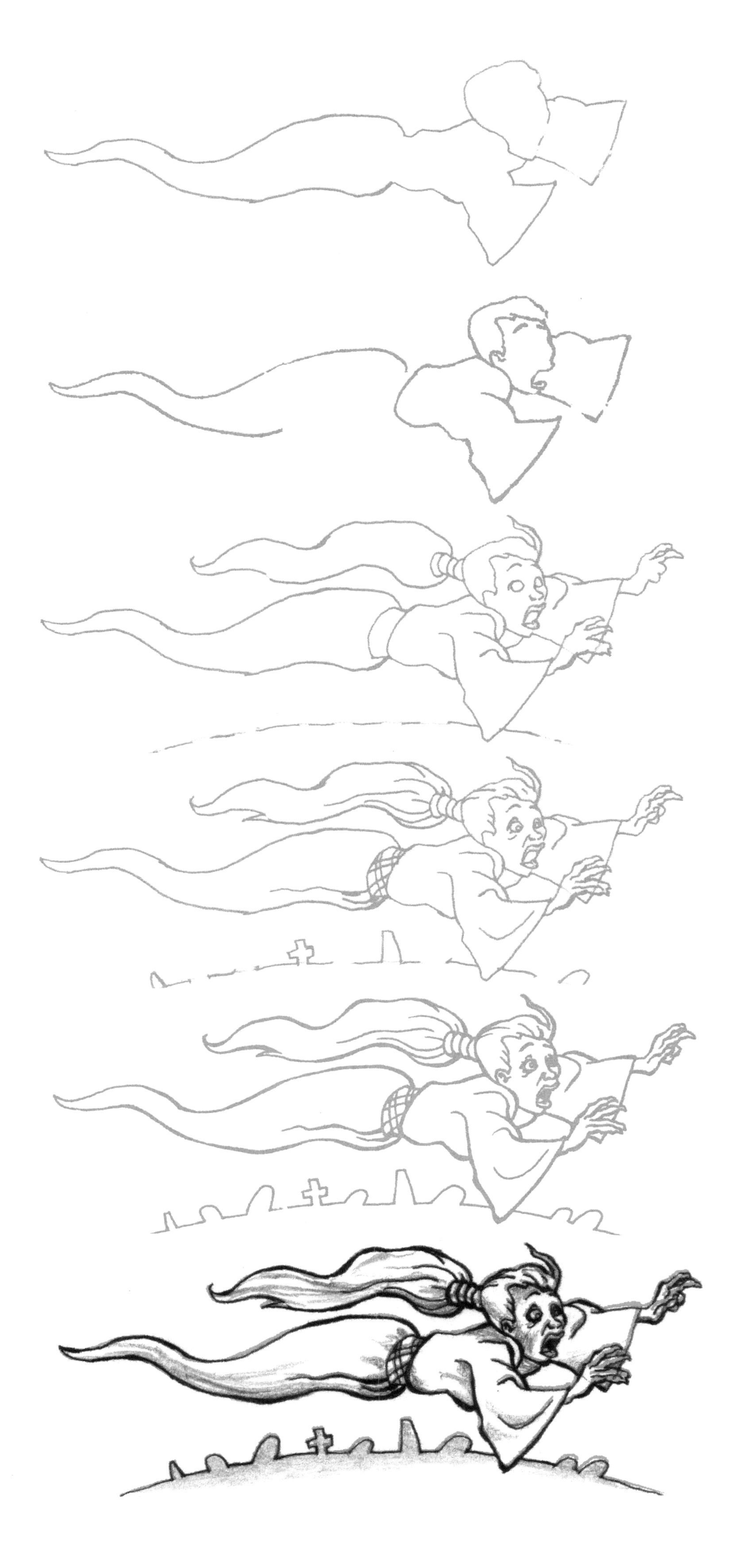

Banshee

Basilisk

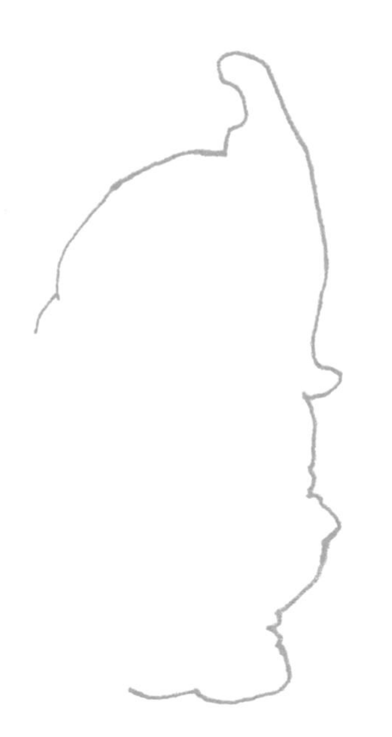
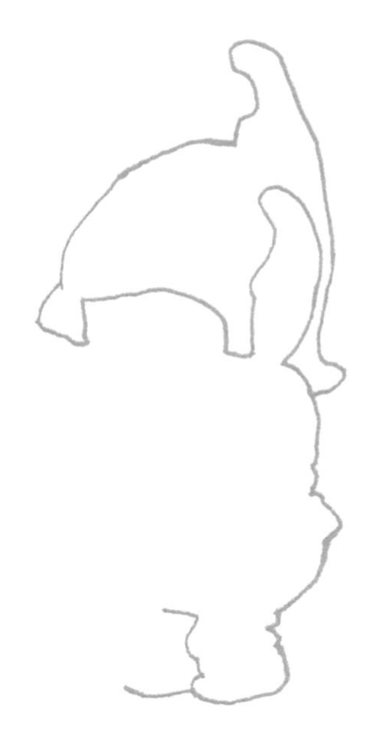

Brownie

Centaur

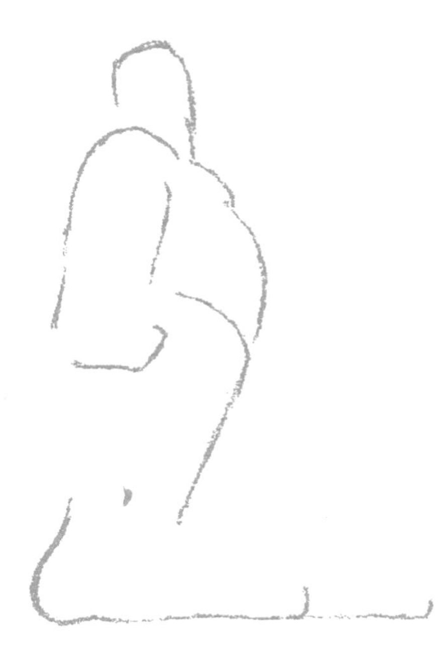

Cyclops

Harpy

Hydra

Medusa

Pegasus

Minotaur

Siren

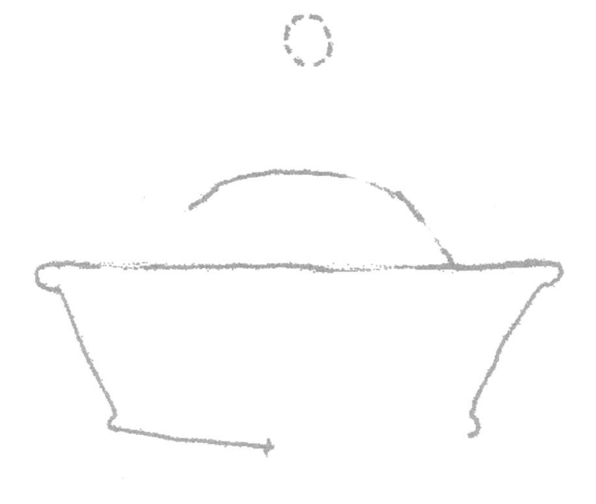

Changeling

Troll

Giant

Gnome

Dwarf

Elf

Fairy

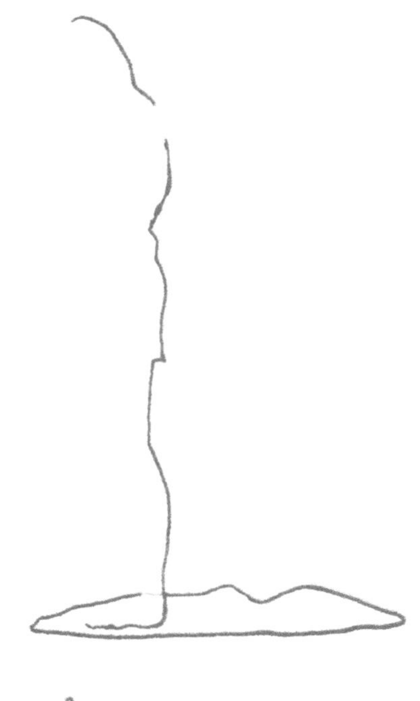

Water Fairy

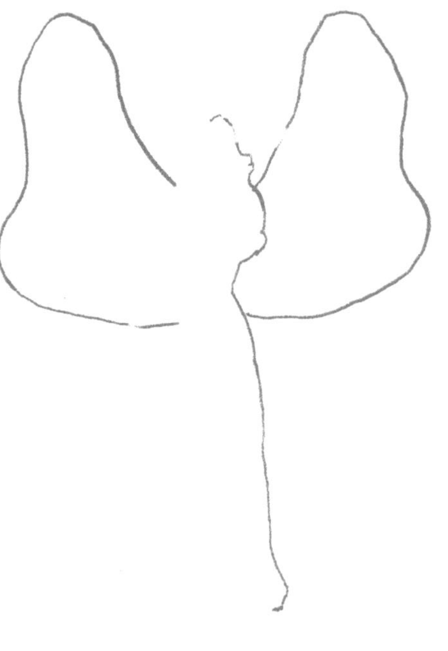

Fairy Queen

Fire-Breathing Dragon

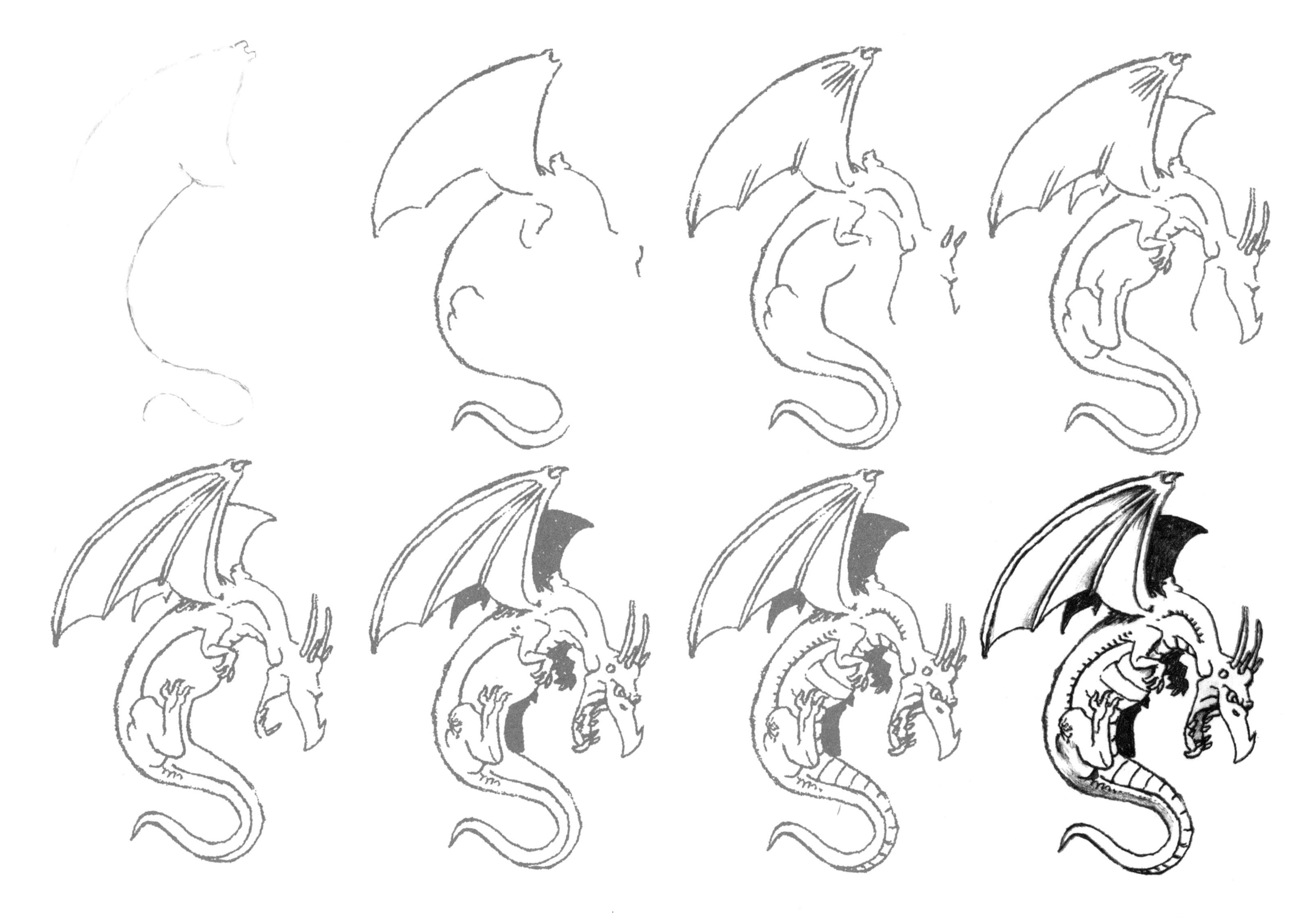

Flying Dragon

Gargoyle

Genie

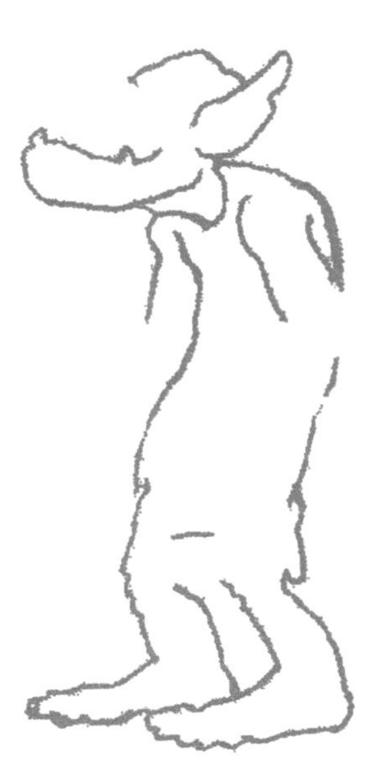

Goblin

Gryphon

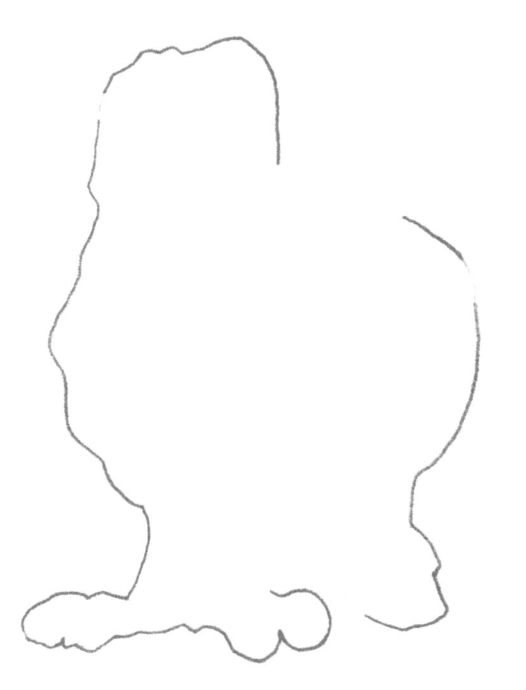

Hippogriff

Imp

Kobold

Leprechaun

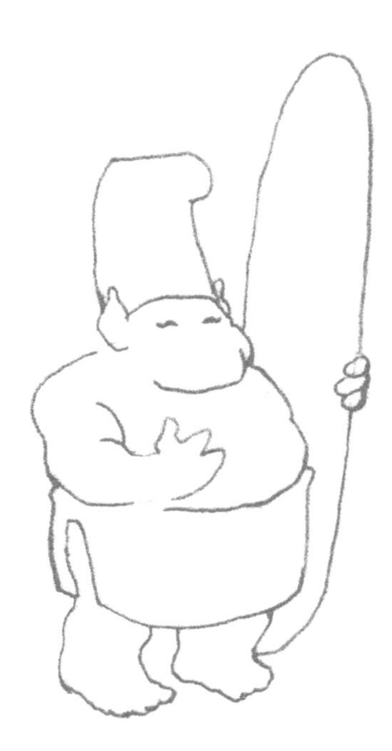

Menehune

Mermaid

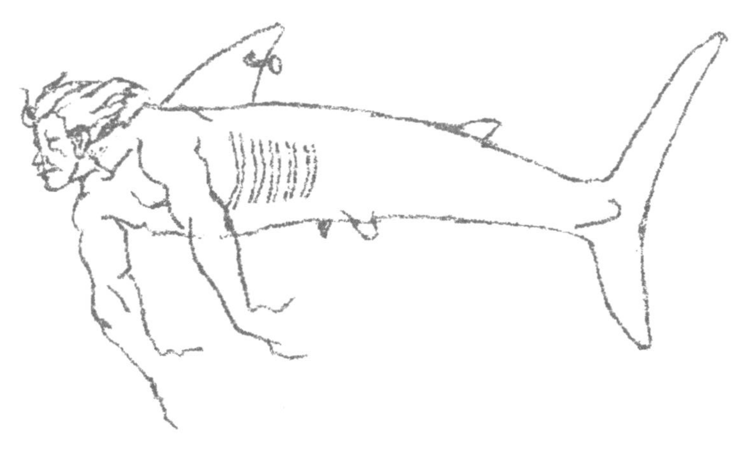

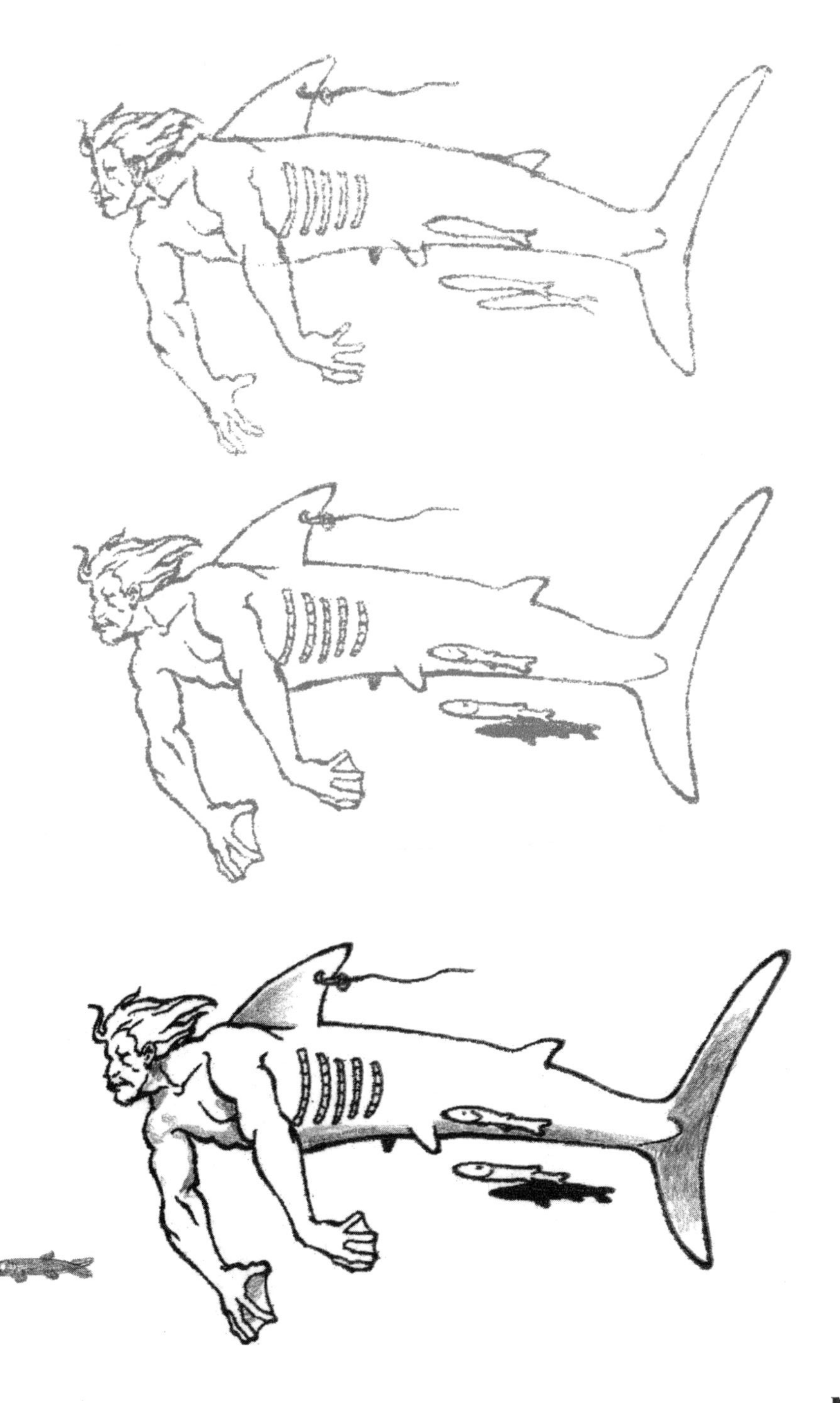

Merman

Sea Serpent

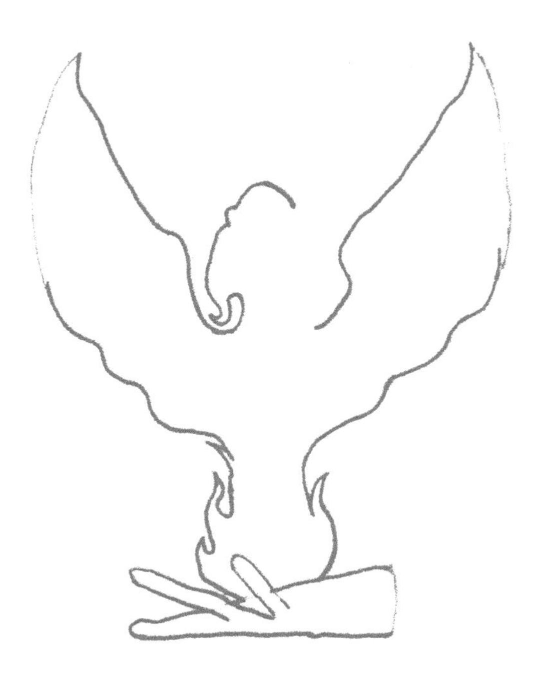

Phoenix

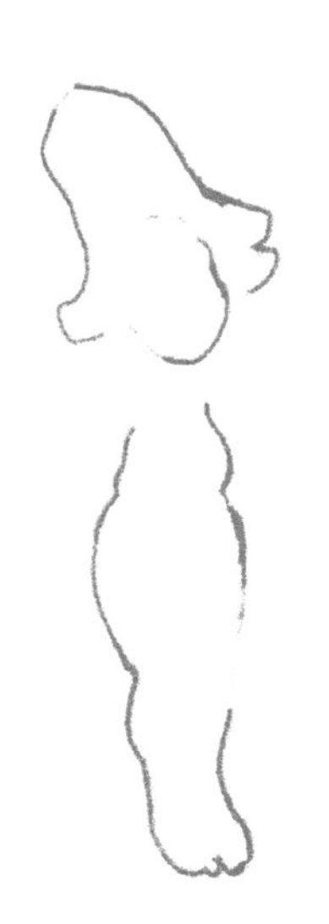

Pixie

Satyr

Sprite

Golem

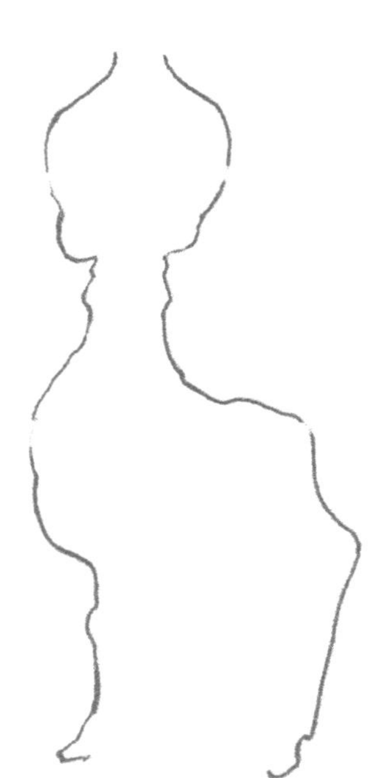
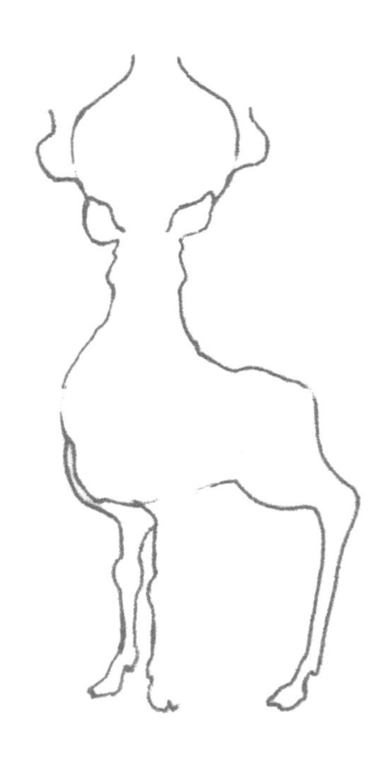

Golden Stag

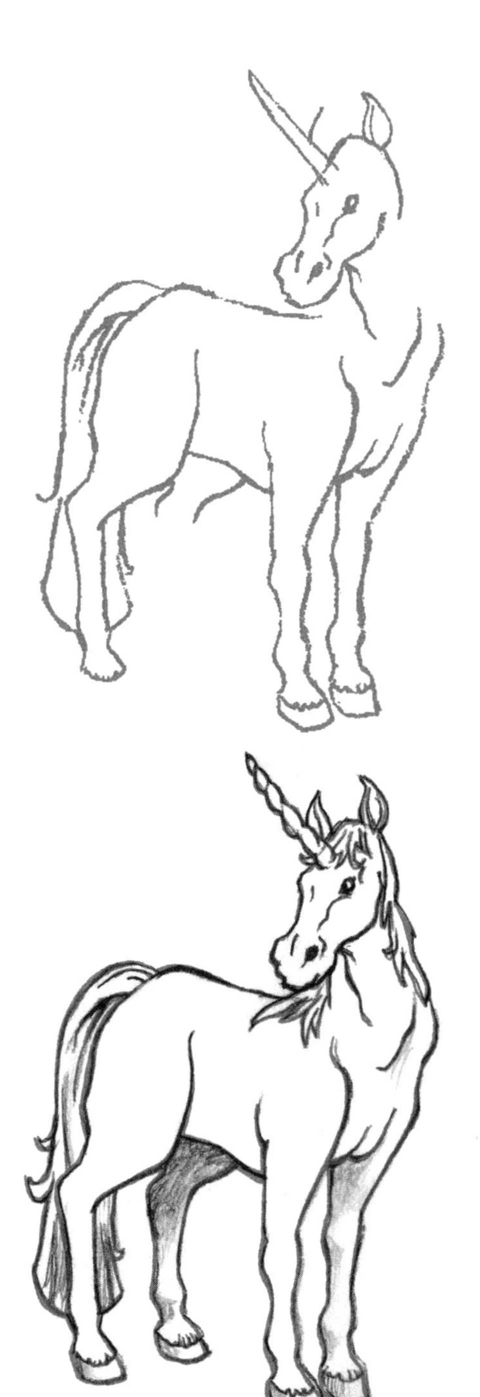

Unicorn

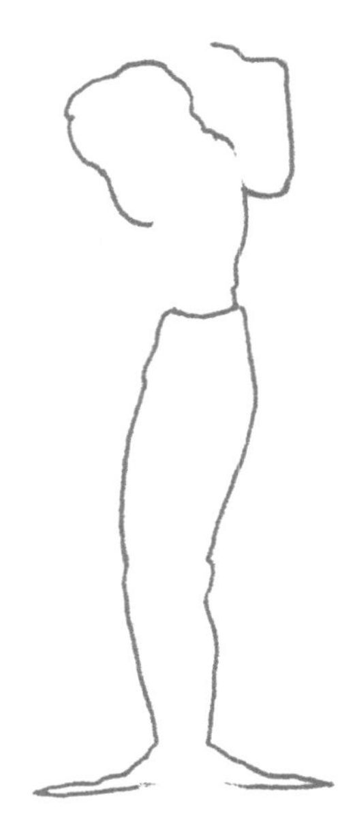
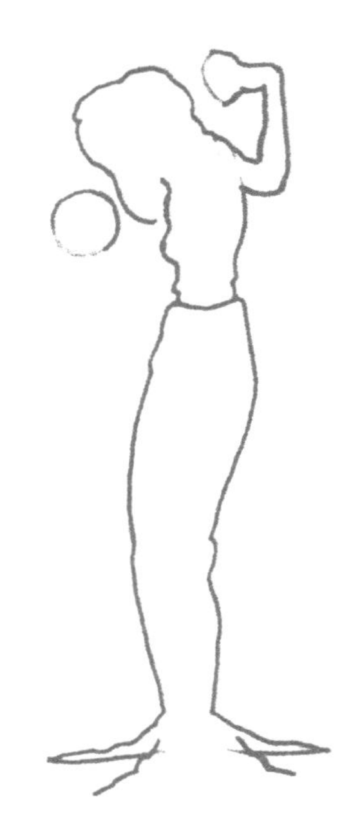

Sorceress

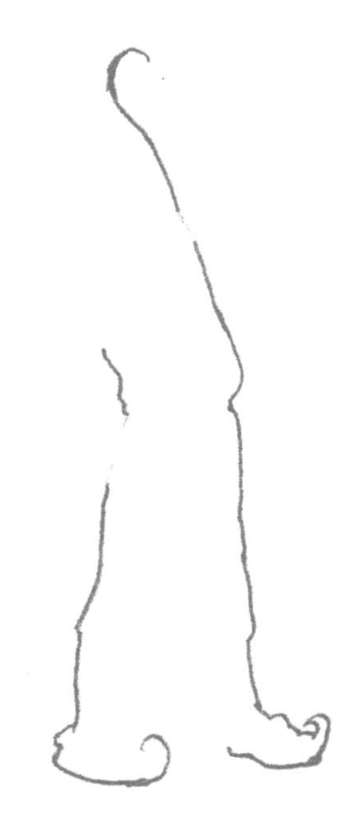

Wizard

Yeti

ABOUT LEE J. AMES

I've been married to Jocelyn for sixty-four years (either I'm lucky or I must have been doing something right). I have a son, Jonathan (his wife's name is Cynthia), and a daughter, Alison (her husband is Marty). I have three grandkids named Mark, Lauren, and Hilary. And I dare not omit our two magnificent hybrid canines, Missy and Rosie. All of the above are the makings of my lovely adventure!

Me? At eighteen I got my first job, at the Walt Disney Studios. Counting travel time across the country, that job lasted three months. I've been cashing in on the glory ever since! I've worked in animation, advertising, comic books, teaching, and illustrating books (about 150). I'm the author of more than thirty-five books (mostly the Draw 50 series). All have helped me happily avoid facing reality. We now live in the paradise of Southern California, but I still maintain membership in the Berndt Toast Gang, New York's chapter of the National Cartoonists Society.